# PERSONAL BEST
# SWIMM

### ROY WILLIAMS

William Collins Sons & Co Ltd
London . Glasgow . Sydney . Auckland
Toronto . Johannesburg

First published by William Collins 1988
© Mander Gooch Callow 1988

ISBN 0-00-194706-0

Printed in Great Britain
by Warners (Midlands) plc

Designed and produced by
MANDER GOOCH CALLOW
Illustrations: Roger Wade-Walker
Front Cover Photograph:
Spectrum Colour Library

# Contents

SWIMMING FOR FUN ....... 4

TRAINING ....................... 6

AT THE POOLSIDE ........... 7

DISTANCE SWIMMING ...... 9

THE BACKSTROKE ......... 11

THE BUTTERFLY ............. 18

THE BREASTSTROKE ..... 23

THE FREESTYLE ............ 26

TEAM CHARTS .............. 30

# Introduction

In these pages you will find 25 games and exercises, with 40 full colour illustrations, specially designed to show you how to make the most of your swimming talents and improve your skills. You will find out all you need to know, from how to plan your training and what to wear, to becoming as sleek as a dolphin in the water and prepared for competition training. You don't need any special equipment, just lots of energy and enthusiasm and of course, to be able to swim!

How do you know you are improving? Well, there are charts and record pages for you to mark and record your very own personal best in each group of skills, so you can see your progress. You can keep a record of the progress of your school or local swimming club too, or even that of the National teams.

You can improve your swimming abilities and have fun at the same time and more importantly, achieve your very own personal best.

# SWIMMING FOR FUN

Swimming is good fun and the best all round exercise for people of all ages, shapes and sizes. It is also one of the few sports in which there are lots of high level races and competitions for children.

## LEARNING TO SWIM

It is very important for everyone to learn to swim. It is a skill which could save your own, or someone else's life one day.

You MUST learn to swim if you want to take part in water sports, like wind-surfing, sail-boarding, water-skiing, canoeing or sailing, even though you will be wearing a life-jacket and head protection if necessary.

You should be taught to swim by a qualified instructor. If you are worried about the water, he or she will be able to help you and give you all important confidence. Most of you will be able to swim already and will be interested in improving your strokes, stamina and fitness for competition swimming.

## SAFETY FIRST

Before you begin you must ask your mum or dad if they are happy about your plans to swim. Sometimes children with ear, nose or throat problems should not go into the water. Although many asthma sufferer's have found that swimming can help their breathing problems.

But your parents may want to check that your doctor approves before you start.

## SWIMMING IN COMPETITION

You may belong to a swimming club at your school or local pool. If not, try to find a pool which has a club with coaching for your age- group. The coach at the club will be able to advise you on a training programme and help you to improve your technique. He will also have all the rules and regulations of competition swimming. It is very important that you learn these from the beginning. Many young swimmers are disappointed later, when they have come first in a race but are disqualified for breaking a rule.

For instance, both hands must touch the wall at the same moment on all turns and at the finish in breaststroke and butterfly. You would be surprised at how many young swimmers don't learn this when they begin their competition swimming.

The games, training programmes and exercises in this book are aimed at improving your skills. You can do them by yourself (it is never advisable to swim alone) or with your friends and take your improved skills back to your club or school. The games are to help swimmers who are very keen to swim in competition. If you are serious about your swimming there are one or two questions to ask yourself.

Do you love swimming, and are you ready to work very, very hard to succeed? Training can be fun, especially if you belong to a club, but it is also a lot of hard and sometimes lonely work. You must remember that doing your best and seeing a big improvement will be a great feeling.

## HOW TO COMPETE
The best way to start to compete is through your own school or club. You will find that a club can arrange for its own members to compete against one another at six years of age. However the Amateur Swimming Association has rules to protect very young children from being made to compete. The minimum ages for inter-club events are as follows.

## NO MINIMUM AGE
Events restricted to members of one club.

## 9 YEARS OLD
(i) Open relay races other than in District and National competitions.
(ii) Inter-club events limited to not more than eight clubs which do not form part of a series of events as in a league.

## 10 YEARS OLD
(i) Open individual events, other than in District and National Competitions.
(ii) Relay events in District Competitions.

## 11 YEARS OLD
(i) Individual events in District Competitions.
(ii) Relay events in National Competitions.

## 12 YEARS OLD
Individual events in National Competitions.
For all categories, the age shall be the age in the year of competition.

## THE POOL
If you don't already belong to a club, it is important to find a pool where the manager will be helpful to you in your training. He must make sure that a lifeguard is on duty when you and your friends' are training. It is a good idea to ask when is the best time for you to go to the pool. Most pools are very busy during the day, but he may allow you to come after school. Ask him if he can arrange to put up lane ropes too, so that you can practice.

Swimming pools up and down the country are of different lengths. It is important that you find out the length of your pool, so that you can vary the games and exercises given here. They are based on a 25 metre pool.

# TRAINING

## SWIMMING EQUIPMENT

You will need to have at least two bathing suits. These should be made of light-weight lycra. It is very important to keep yourself warm before and after training, especially in cold weather. So you will also need two large bath towels and a tracksuit. Try to have a good pair of training shoes, a pair of 'flip-flops', and a swimming cap. Some pool managers insist on caps for all bathers.

The most important piece of equipment is a swimming float. They come in different sizes and materials. The best size and material will depend on your size. Go to your local sports shop and ask for help in choosing the right one for your size and weight.

The float is very important in training, because it helps you to streamline your body position in the water. It also helps when you learn breathing technique practices with your coach. Competitive swimmers use them while they are doing legs only or arms only training. So don't forget, keep your float with you at all times during training. If you don't have to wear goggles, it is better not to do so when you are training.

## WHAT TO EAT

Most children are fit and healthy. When you are training hard, you burn up lots of calories. It is important to eat plenty of fresh food which is high in protein to build you up. Foods which are high in protein are meat, fish and fresh fruit and vegetables. The National Coach Federation advises as wide a diet as possible. The recommend eating six different fruits or vegetables daily. Most important of all is milk. Try not to eat too many sweets, cakes and biscuits. They stop you feeling hungry but the effect doesn't last and they don't help to build muscle and bone.

## WHEN TO EAT

It is very important that you never eat your main meals before training. If you have a large meal before you go into the water, you may get cramp which is very dangerous. Also you will be hungry after training as you burn up lots of calories and need to take nourishment then.

## SLEEP

You are probably getting plenty of sleep already, but when you are training hard you will need at least 8-9 hours sleep each night. Make sure you always have a good rest following a long training session.

## WHEN TO TRAIN

Adult swimmers do the main part of their training early in the morning, before breakfast and after a good night's sleep. But training twice a day, which usually involves early morning sessions is not advised for children. Once a day should be enough.

# AT THE POOLSIDE

## STRETCHING
Before you even think about getting into the water it is very, very important that you stretch your muscles properly. If you have seen swimming competitions on the television, you will have noticed that the swimmers always do stretching exercises before they get into the water. It is very important to stretch all the right muscles and set the posture of your body before you start swimming. Here are some simple stretches. We call the swimmers in our drawings, Andrew and Clare.

## HIP CIRCLES
Clare stands up straight with her feet about 23 cms apart. Her hands are on her hips. She swings her hips to the side. Then she swings them around to the back. Then to the other side and finally, forwards in a circular movement.

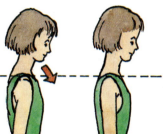
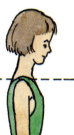

## SHOULDER CIRCLES
Clare stands with her feet about 23 cms apart. She keeps her arms down by her sides. She lifts her shoulders up, and moves them in a circle, inwards towards her neck (anti-clockwise). She keeps her arms straight but relaxed all the time. She does this 10-15 times, then she repeats the exercise. This time she moves her shoulders outwards (clockwise).

Try to do this 15-20 times.

## KNEES TO CHEST

Clare stands perfectly upright. She bends her right arm in front of her. She brings her left knee up to her right elbow. She is careful to bring her KNEE UP and not her ELBOW DOWN. She then brings her right knee up to her left elbow. Then left knee to right elbow and so on, until each elbow is touched 10 times.

## WAIST TWISTS

Andrew stands with his feet about 46 cms apart. He twists his body, from the waist, as far round as he can. He keeps his hips still and facing forwards.
Try to do this 15-20 times.

## SIDE BENDS

Andrew stands up straight with his feet about 46 cms apart. He is careful not to bend forwards or backwards during this exercise. He reaches down the left-hand side of his leg with his left hand. He keeps his right arm straight. He does this 15-20 times. Then he repeats the exercise with his right arm, 15-20 times.

# *DISTANCE SWIMMING*

## STAMINA

Before you learn to make all your swimming strokes perfect, it is important to build up your strength and stamina You will need to be able to swim distances.

You cannot expect to get into the pool and swim 60 lengths straight away. You need to build up slowly. Do not push yourself too hard. If at any time you feel sick or dizzy, stop at once and rest.
Your aim is to build up to 1500 metres, which sounds like a very long distance. Most pools are 25 metres long, so this will be 60 lengths of the pool. If you are already quite good at swimming you will not find it too difficult to manage 30 lengths. If you could add a length a day you would have reached your 60 lengths in a month. If you are starting at 20 lengths, than it will take about 6 weeks to build up to 60 lengths. If you begin on 10, it will take you about 7-8 weeks and so on. The plan we are working with here will imagine that you are starting on 30 lengths. We will also imagine that you are doing one training session a day.

Most competitive swimmers use the freestyle stroke. Lots of children are taught the breaststroke from the beginning. In fact it is a much harder stroke to get right than the freestyle. If you can, start your distance swimming in freestyle. It is a good idea to avoid distance swimming in breaststroke because it can give you knee problems later on, because of over-use. At this stage, it is your aim to build up distance.

### DISTANCE CHART
Number of Lengths per day

| | Day 1 | Day 2 | Day 3 | Day 4 | Day 5 | Day 6 | Day 7 | |
|---|---|---|---|---|---|---|---|---|
| Week 1 | ......... | ......... | ......... | ......... | ......... | ......... | ......... | PERSONAL BEST |
| Week 2 | ......... | ......... | ......... | ......... | ......... | ......... | ......... | PERSONAL BEST |
| Week 3 | ......... | ......... | ......... | ......... | ......... | ......... | ......... | PERSONAL BEST |
| Week 4 | ......... | ......... | ......... | ......... | ......... | ......... | ......... | PERSONAL BEST |
| Week 5 | ......... | ......... | ......... | ......... | ......... | ......... | ......... | PERSONAL BEST |

## SPEED

When you can swim 60 lengths comfortably, lets say after 30 days of 1 hour sessions. You should be able to get the distance in under an hour, about 50 minutes.

Now we want to improve your speed. So your second month's aim will be to try to take 10 minutes off the time it takes you to swim the 60 lengths. That sounds a lot, but it is really only about 10-15 seconds a day.

By now you should be a better swimmer and a stronger swimmer. It sounds very hard work indeed but it is possible. Mum or Dad are probably very pleased with your progress. Perhaps they or a friend will help by timing your swim and you can then use the chart to keep a record of the distance you manage and the time in which you swim it.

If you are training by yourself do not try to do 'land training'. This is very complicated and should not be attempted without the guidance of a coach. So wait until you belong to a club before you start. There are lots of things you can do to improve your swimming by yourself.

## SPEED CHART

Time for each length/time for each distance

| | Day 1 | Day 2 | Day 3 | Day 4 | Day 5 | Day 6 | Day 7 | |
|---|---|---|---|---|---|---|---|---|
| Week 1 | .................... | .................... | .................... | .................... | .................... | .................... | .................... | PERSONAL BEST |
| Week 2 | .................... | .................... | .................... | .................... | .................... | .................... | .................... | PERSONAL BEST |
| Week 3 | .................... | .................... | .................... | .................... | .................... | .................... | .................... | PERSONAL BEST |
| Week 4 | .................... | .................... | .................... | .................... | .................... | .................... | .................... | PERSONAL BEST |
| Week 5 | .................... | .................... | .................... | .................... | .................... | .................... | .................... | PERSONAL BEST |

# THE STROKES

You are a far better swimmer than you were at the beginning because of your own very hard work and distance swimming, which has made you much stronger. Once you have built up your stamina and speed over 60 lengths you will be ready to start learning stroke and breathing technique. There are four strokes recognised in competition. These are backstroke, butterfly, breaststroke and freestyle. You must be able to swim all four strokes comfortably, if you want to compete. Then you can choose your favourite stroke. We will learn how to make the strokes properly and the correct breathing technique for each. It is important to do this early.

# THE BACKSTROKE

### BY THE POOL
Remember to stretch well with your stretching exercises. In the first games the swimmers keep their arms straight. You may have seen good swimmers in competition with their arms bent slightly and under the water. This will come at a later stage. For now, it is important that both your arms come up straight and enter the water straight. Practise each stage of the stroke separately and then put them together in the stroke. Make sure you have a least ten to fifteen minutes to spare each week for the backstroke practice.

 **GAME 1**

**STRAIGHT ARM LIFTS**
for 1 swimmer

Do this on the pool side. Andrew stands up straight, with his chin up. He puts his left arm out straight in front of him. His palm is turned outwards. He brings his arm up slowly towards his ear. He holds his arm in the same position with his palm outwards.
He brings his arm right back in this position, towards his legs. Then he does the same with his right arm, then left again and so on.
Do this ten times with alternate arms.

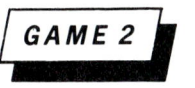

## WALKING BACKWARDS
for 1 swimmer

Andrew gets into the shallow end of the pool. When the water reaches his waist, he stands upright with his chin up. He puts his left arm straight out in front of him.

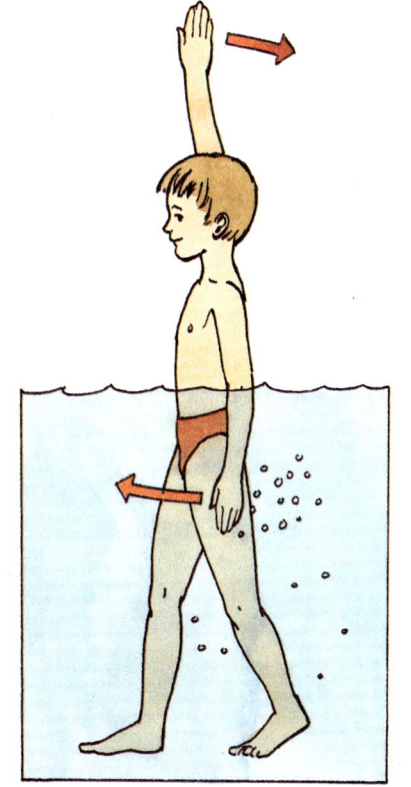

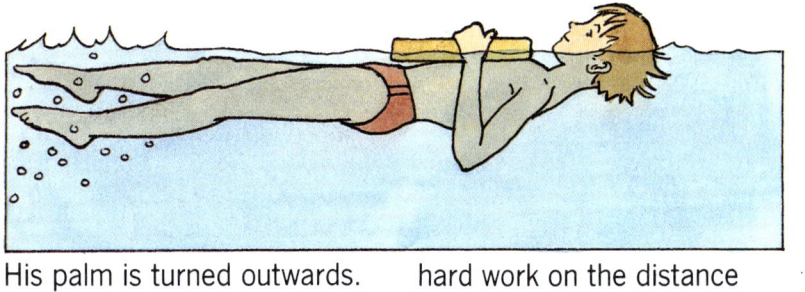

His palm is turned outwards. He brings his arm up towards his ear and then back and down towards his leg. He keeps his arm straight all the time. Then he does the same with his right arm, then left and so on. As he brings first his left and then his right arm backwards, arm straight, palms outwards, he walks backwards width-wise across the pool. He makes sure that both his arms are doing the same thing and remain straight.
Try to do this for 10 widths.

### LEG ACTION
For this practice you will need your swimming float.
Make sure that your body is flat on the water and very streamlined. Your body should be so flat that the water covers your ears. After your

hard work on the distance swims your kicking technique should be very strong. It is essential that your backstroke kicking is both comfortable and strong, before you start the arm movements of this stroke.

### GAME 3    FLOAT KICKS
for 1 swimmer

Andrew is streamlined in the water. The water covers his ears. He puts his float flat on his chest, tucking it up under his chin. He pushes off from the side of the pool, using both feet and swims width-wise across the pool. He only uses his legs. His toes just touch the surface of the water. He makes sure that his float is fixed on his chest at all times.
Try to do this for 6 widths.

### GAME 4

## ONE ARM KICKS
for 1 swimmer

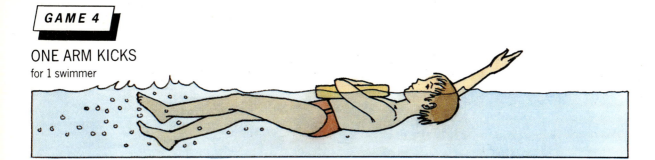

In the water, Andrew holds the float across his chest with one arm. He pushes himself off hard from the side. He brings the other arm straight out of the water, palm outwards, around by his ear and down towards his leg. At the same time, he kicks his legs. He swims width-wise across the pool. When he reaches the side he changes arms and swims back across the pool. On every width, he changes arms.
Try to do this for 8 widths.

When you have mastered the first four games, you are ready to try an exercise that is a little harder. Remember you are still working width-wise. It is essential that you keep both legs straight and very tightly together, for this practice.

### HIGH SKILL PRACTICE

Andrew stands up in the water and put the float in between his legs. He lies back gently. Then, using both arms in the action he has been practising (above), he pushes himself off and moves width-wise across the pool. He keeps his arm movements slow, so that he creates less swell in the water.

After two to three weeks of width practice, do exactly the same exercise only length-wise.
Now swim the full-stroke, length-wise down the pool.

# HIGH SKILL PRACTICE

Each length will begin with a BACKSTROKE START and each turn will be a BACKSTROKE TUMBLE.

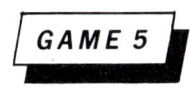

**GAME 5**

## BACKSTROKE START
for 1 swimmer

Andrew starts off by holding on to the edge of the pool with both hands. His arms are shoulder-width apart and straight. He puts both feet on the side of the pool, just below the water surface. His stronger foot is slightly lower.

His feet are about hip-width apart. He bends his elbows and pulls his body upwards and inwards. His back is rounded and his chest is close to his knees. His knees break the surface of the water between his bent arms. He

presses downwards. He lifts his hips clear of the water. At the same time he lifts his body upwards and away from the side. He brings his head upwards and backwards. He swings his straight arms sideways and backwards, and pushes his legs straight with as much force as he can. As he pushes off he stretches and slightly arches his back.

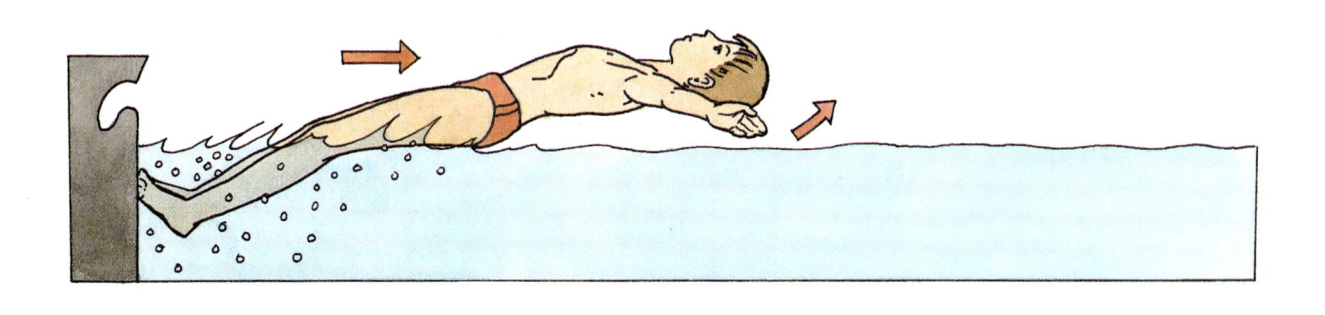

He puts his head between his outstretched arms. He breathes in. Then he stretches from his fingertips to his toes holding his head back and between his arms. He brings his arms together and keeps as low as possible. He keeps his arms fully stretched, hands close together, fingers pointing. His head, back and hips are up. He streamlines his body just under the water surface, keeping it as near to horizontal as he can. He breathes out through his nose while underwater. He glides for a short distance by which time he reaches swimming speed. He then gives a dolphin kick, then pulls with one arm. His head comes forward and breaks the surface of the water as his pulling arm is ready for the stroke and his other arm is ready to pull.

Try to do 5 backstroke starts.

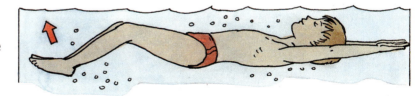

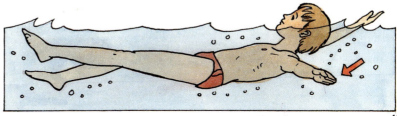

## GAME 6

### BACKSTROKE TUMBLE
for 1 swimmer

When Andrew comes to the end of his length, he breathes in and stretches his leading arm towards the wall as he reaches it.
He looks backwards, keeping his head back. He touches the wall, under the surface, with his palm, his hand is flat. Then his fingers point downwards and inwards. He reaches down and in front of his head and holds his trailing arm down by his side. As his leading arm touches the wall he bends it, tucks his legs and thrusts his knees upwards. He lifts and throws his legs sideways, over the surface towards the arm which is touching the wall. He keeps his knees close together and pushes his body around his leading arm.

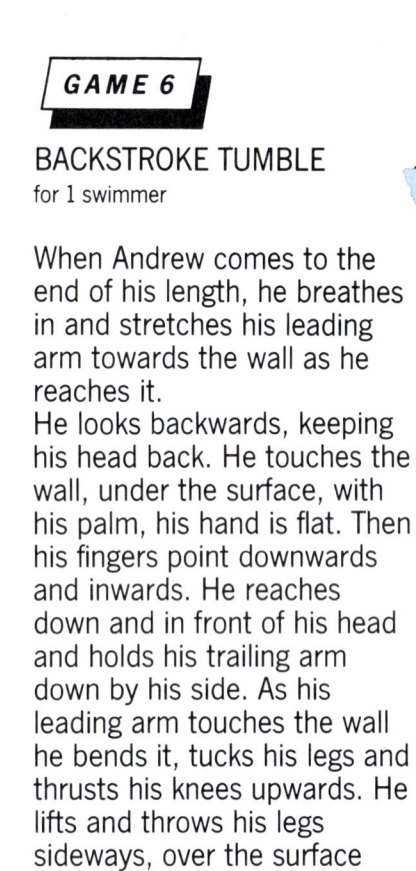

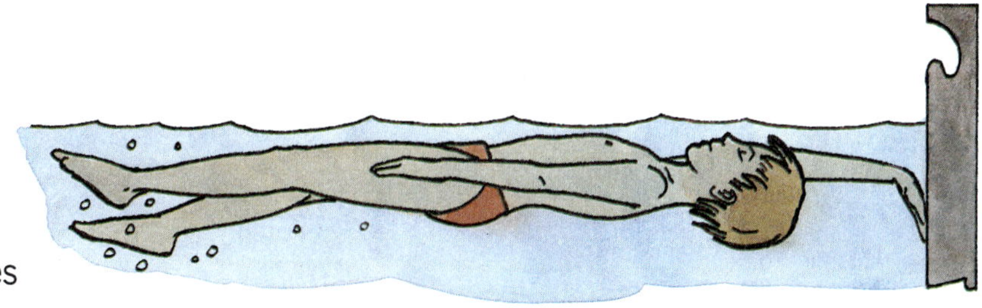

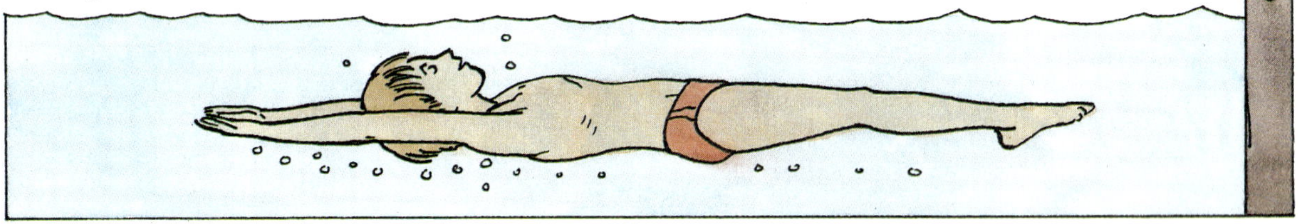

He pushes and straightens his arm. At the same time, he is pulling his trailing arm upwards with his hand towards his head. He turns his body with his chest facing upwards, staying flat on his back. As he turns, he brings his hands together above his head. He straightens his arms and pushes his legs, keeping his head between his arms. He drives away from the side and stretches from his fingertips to his toes.

## BREATHING
For the backstroke you breathe in through your mouth whilst your arms and legs are between stroke actions and out through your nose and mouth during the stroke.

When you can do the full stroke lengthwise down the pool with backstroke starts and backstroke tumble turns. You can start to build up speed and distance. Try and build up your distance to four lengths of backstroke and time them. Then you can begin to concentrate on bringing your time down by a fraction each length.

BACKSTROKE CHART

| | | | | | |
|---|---|---|---|---|---|
| GAME 1 | Date ......... | Goal ......... | Date ......... | Goal ......... | Date ......... |
| GAME 2 | Date ......... | Goal ......... | Date ......... | Goal ......... | Date ......... |
| GAME 3 | Date ......... | Goal ......... | Date ......... | Goal ......... | Date ......... |
| GAME 4 | Date ......... | Goal ......... | Date ......... | Goal ......... | Date ......... |
| Backstroke Starts | Date ......... | Goal ......... | Date ......... | Goal ......... | Date ......... |
| Backstroke Tumbles | Date ......... | Goal ......... | Date ......... | Goal ......... | Date ......... |

# THE BUTTERFLY

## IN THE POOL

For practice in the butterfly we will go straight into the water and we will do it without the float.

You will find that you will learn the stroke more quickly and get the rhythm of the stroke better without using a float. Remember to stretch well before you start.

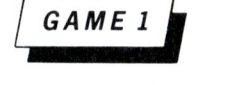

## TWO ARM SWINGS
for 1 swimmer

Clare stands up straight, waist high in the water. She lifts both arms straight in front of her. She pushes them down towards the water. She keeps pushing down through the water, until her arms can go no further. She turns the palms of her hands upwards. She uses her shoulders to bring her arms over and around, so they pass her ears. She brings them back to their starting position. She does this about 20 times.

Then she does the same exercise, but this time she puts her face in the water. She breathes in through her mouth when she feels she needs to and out as slowly as she can. At this stage she does this whenever she needs to.

Try to do this 20 times.

| GAME 2 | **ARM WIDTHS**
for 1 swimmer

Clare is now ready to cross the pool width-wise. She takes a deep breath and pushes off from the side. She brings her arms up and over as in Game 1. She tries to get as far across the pool as she can. She does not worry too much about her feet. She is practising her arm movements. At first she is breathing in through her mouth and blowing out slowly when she needs to. Sometimes this is once a stroke and sometimes 4 times. Try to do 2 complete widths.

TIP Don't forget this stroke starts at the front.
When you can complete two widths of the pool you are ready to master the breathing technique.

BREATHING
At first it is best to do this exercise standing at chest height in the water. Do the arm movements for the stroke with your face in the water. Take a deep breath at the beginning of each stroke and blow out as slowly as you can. Make sure your head is held still once it has entered the water. When you can take one breath for each complete stroke, work width-wise across the pool, practising your breathing technique with your arm stroke. Concentrate on your arms and breathing, later you will learn the dolphin kick. When you can do two widths with one breath for each stroke, it is best to practise lengthwise in the pool. Try to do 4 lengths.

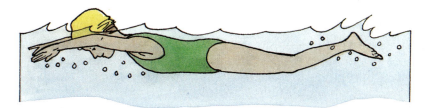

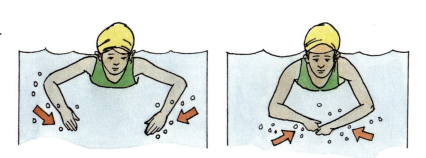

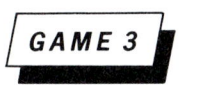

## DOLPHIN KICKING
for 1 swimmer

In this game we develop the kicking action for the Butterfly.

Clare goes to the shallow end of the pool. She holds tight with her hands to the side. She bends her arms slightly and brings both her legs up to the surface of the water. She keeps her knees together and slightly bent. Her legs are straight. She moves both legs up and down vertically in the water. Her hip movements and those of her upper body are comfortable. When she can do this easily she stretches her arms out straight and repeats the exercise.

When this comes easily to you you will be ready for the high skill practice.

### HIGH SKILL PRACTICE

Stand up, waist high, in the water, with your hands down by your sides on your legs. Do not move your arms at all. Take a deep breath, put your face in the water and try a whole width of dolphin kick. When you have gained some more confidence, try the same exercise – this time with your arms stretched in front of you. (Do not attempt to use a float).

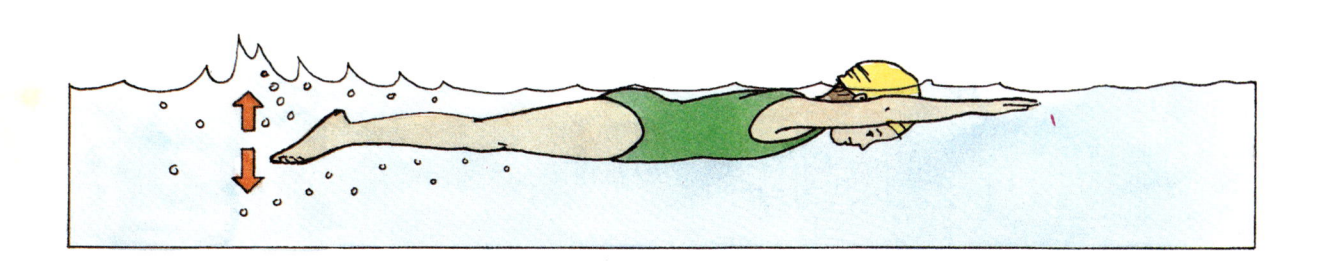

Now it is time to try to combine the breathing with the leg and arm movement width-wise across the pool. When this comes easily to you, swim the full stroke, length-wise. It will take a little while to get a perfect rhythm working. There is no better practice than combining technique and distance. Try for a width of the pool.
When you can do this, try for two widths, then three, then four. Try to reduce the time it takes to swim each length by 10 seconds.

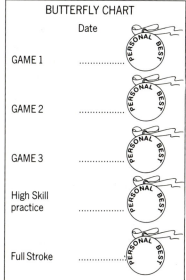

# THE BREASTSTROKE

## RULES AND REGULATIONS

In the past few years, the rules of breaststroke have changed quite a bit. It is very important to make sure that you get the correct rules to begin with and be aware of them when you are competing at any level. For instance: your head must break the surface of the water once in each stroke cycle. Your legs are not allowed to break the surface of the water at any time. Remember too, both your hands must touch at the same time, on all turns and at the finish.

Before you begin the practice, stretch well with your stretching exercises.

## GAME 1

### HEELS IN, TOES OUT
for 1 swimmer

This game is done by the side of the pool.

Andrew sits down with the palms of his hands on the floor, slightly behind him. He is balanced on the base of his spine. He brings both his knees up. His heels are facing each other and his toes are turned outwards. His knees are never more than hip-width apart. He straightens his legs, then brings them together again in his starting position (heels facing, toes turned out).

When you can do this easily move on to a high skill practice.

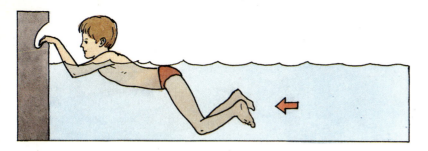
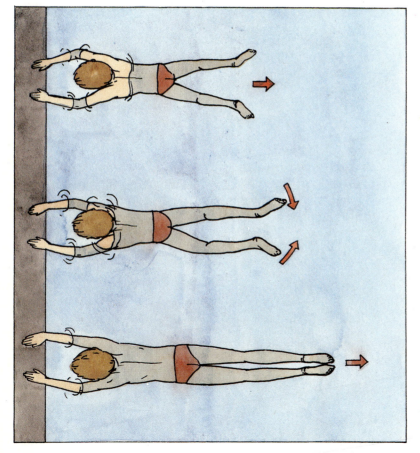

## HIGH SKILL PRACTICE

Enter the pool and hold the side with both hands. To begin with, bend your elbows if it is more comfortable for you. Make sure that both your knees are level in the water and that your heels are together. Your feet should be turned out. Practise straightening your legs and then bringing them back to the starting position. Do not move on to the next game until you can do this easily.

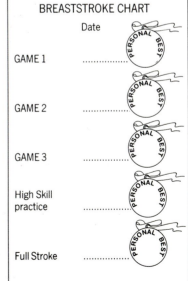

## GAME 2

### HEELS IN, TOES OUT – WIDTHS
for 1 swimmer

Andrew stands upright, waist high in the water. He stretches his arms out in front of him and keeps them absolutely still. He takes a deep breath, blows out slowly and tries to go as far as he can across the pool. He is bringing his heels together, toes turned out and doing the breaststroke kick.

Try to do do four widths.

When he can do four widths, Andrew practises his breast stroke kick length-wise as well. He uses his float to keep his arms absolutely still and develop a strong kick.

### BREATHING
Breaststroke breathing technique is very similar to the butterfly, that is, in through your mouth at the beginning of the stroke and out slowly through your nose and mouth, building in force during the rest of the stroke. You should breathe once every stroke, but in the beginning take a breath when you need to. Try to build up so that you only take one breath for every stroke.

## GAME 3

### ARM MOVES
for 1 swimmer

Andrew stands, chest deep in the water with his arms stretched out in front of him. He turns his hands so that the backs are together. He pulls his arms out slowly to the sides a few centimetres under the surface of the water. When his arms are just over shoulder-width apart, he bends them at his elbows and gently brings his hands towards each other. He pushes out in front. When he can do this easily he combines the arm and leg movements across the pool width-wise.

Try to do six widths at a time.

When this comes easily to you, begin to build up your distance over lengths of the pool. Try to take one breath for every stroke.
When this is also easy, try to reduce the time it takes you to swim each length by 10 seconds. Aim for 20 lengths of the pool in the shortest possible time.

# THE FREESTYLE

## STRENGTH, STAMINA, DISTANCE

The freestyle is the most popular stroke of all. Most children prefer to swim this stroke. If it is your favourite stroke then that will be an added bonus for this part of your training. Most competitive swimmers use freestyle to build up stamina and strength for the other strokes. They also swim most of their distance training in freestyle. Remember to stretch first.

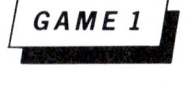

## FLIPPER KICKS
for 1 swimmer

Clare starts off in the water at the edge of the pool. She holds on to the side with both hands. Her arms are stretched out and her chin is in the water. She keeps her legs straight with a very slight bend at her knees. Her toes are kept well back and very relaxed, from her ankle right

down through her foot. She pretends that instead of two feet she has a pair of flippers at the end of her legs. She kicks in an up and down

movement, both legs moving smoothly without breaking the pattern. That is one moves down as the other moves up and so on.

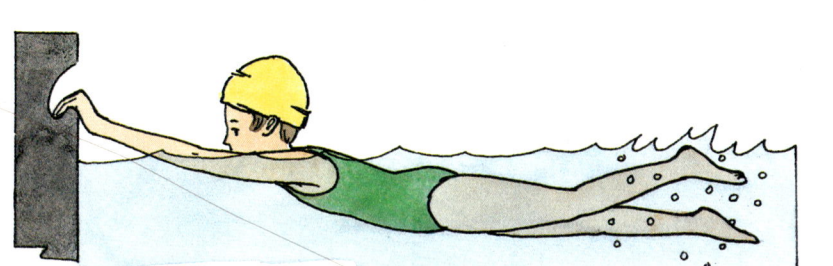

TIP REMEMBER that the biggest splash doesn't mean that you are doing the exercise correctly. Your heels must just reach the surface of the water.

| GAME 2 | **OVER ARMS**
for 1 player

Clare stands waist-high in the water. She keeps her arms straight out in front of her. She reaches down into the water with her left arm. As her arm enters the water, her wrist is firm. Her arm pulls along the centre line of her body. When her arm is in the water, it doesn't pull down in a dead straight line. Half way down through the stroke she bends her arm as if she were writing the letter 'S' with her hand. She then does the same with her right arm, then her left and so on.

## HIGH SKILL PRACTICE

When you can do both the arm and leg movements easily, practise both separately for the width of the pool. Put the float between your legs and practise the arm motion. Then hold the float out in front of you and practise the leg action. Try to do four widths of each.

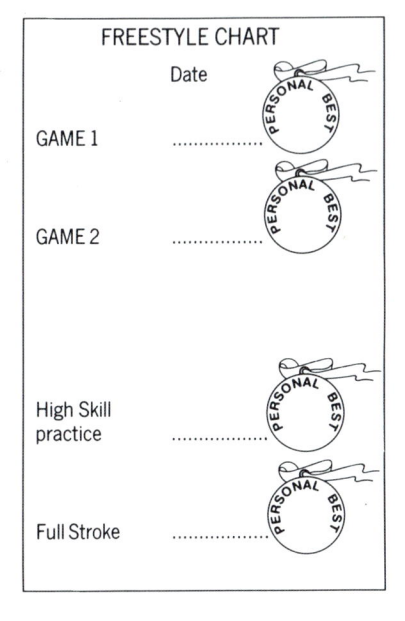

FREESTYLE CHART

Date

GAME 1 ...................

GAME 2 ...................

High Skill
practice ...................

Full Stroke ...................

When you have reached your goal for the widths, build up the same arm only and leg only exercises over lengths. Try to do 4 lengths of each.

Remember how you built up your distance swimming in breaststroke to 60 lengths (1500 metres).
Try to do that and more if possible, with this stroke, because this is the stroke that you will use most.

BREATHING
There are about four versions of breathing technique in this stroke. You may have been taught one or another. You should keep to one and that is taking one breath for every stroke. You will take a breath as your arm comes out of the water in the stroke. Firstly, you must find out which way your head comes out of the water most naturally, when you turn it to the side. Either

to the right or to the left. The best way to find this out is to stand waist high in the water. Take a deep breath and put the whole of your face in the water. When you feel ready to take a breath, let your face come out of the water naturally. If your face comes out of the water to the right, then your right arm will be your breathing arm. If it is to the left, then it will be your left arm.

## THE FULL STROKE

It is very important that everything works towards the centre of your body.
Clare pushes off with both feet from the side of the pool. When her breathing arm comes out of the water, she turns her head from the centre to the right and back. Now she can take a deep breath. As her breathing arm goes back into the water, her head rolls down and she starts blowing out. In the time it takes to take the breath her other arm has made a full circle.

Now as with the other strokes you will need to practise your lengths of the pool, until you can swim smoothly, breathing correctly. Then you must try to reduce the time each length takes by 10 seconds. As we said at the beginning, really improving your strokes with perfect technique, your speed and your stamina is very hard work. It is also great fun and in a very short time you will be able to look at your record charts and be amazed at how you have improved on your 'Personal Best'.
Good Luck!

# TEAM CHART

| Competition | Date | Team | Stroke | Distance | Winner | Time |
|---|---|---|---|---|---|---|
| .................................. | ........................ | ...................... | ..................... | ..................... | ........................... | .................... |
| .................................. | ........................ | ...................... | ..................... | ..................... | ........................... | .................... |
| .................................. | ........................ | ...................... | ..................... | ..................... | ........................... | .................... |
| .................................. | ........................ | ...................... | ..................... | ..................... | ........................... | .................... |
| .................................. | ........................ | ...................... | ..................... | ..................... | ........................... | .................... |
| .................................. | ........................ | ...................... | ..................... | ..................... | ........................... | .................... |
| .................................. | ........................ | ...................... | ..................... | ..................... | ........................... | .................... |
| .................................. | ........................ | ...................... | ..................... | ..................... | ........................... | .................... |
| .................................. | ........................ | ...................... | ..................... | ..................... | ........................... | .................... |
| .................................. | ........................ | ...................... | ..................... | ..................... | ........................... | .................... |

# TEAM CHART

| Competition | Date | Team | Stroke | Distance | Winner | Time |
|---|---|---|---|---|---|---|
| ............................... | ........................ | ........................ | ........................ | ........................ | ........................ | .................... |
| ............................... | ........................ | ........................ | ........................ | ........................ | ........................ | .................... |
| ............................... | ........................ | ........................ | ........................ | ........................ | ........................ | .................... |
| ............................... | ........................ | ........................ | ........................ | ........................ | ........................ | .................... |
| ............................... | ........................ | ........................ | ........................ | ........................ | ........................ | .................... |
| ............................... | ........................ | ........................ | ........................ | ........................ | ........................ | .................... |
| ............................... | ........................ | ........................ | ........................ | ........................ | ........................ | .................... |
| ............................... | ........................ | ........................ | ........................ | ........................ | ........................ | .................... |
| ............................... | ........................ | ........................ | ........................ | ........................ | ........................ | .................... |
| ............................... | ........................ | ........................ | ........................ | ........................ | ........................ | .................... |

# TEAM CHART

| Competition | Date | Team | Stroke | Distance | Winner | Time |
|---|---|---|---|---|---|---|
| | | | | | | |
| | | | | | | |
| | | | | | | |
| | | | | | | |
| | | | | | | |
| | | | | | | |
| | | | | | | |
| | | | | | | |
| | | | | | | |
| | | | | | | |